Just Good Friends

Heather Hacking

Hodder & Stoughton

LONDON SYDNEY AUCKLAND

British Library Cataloguing in Publication Data
A record for this book is available from the British Library

ISBN 0 340 86397 8

Printed and bound in Great Britain by
Bookmarque Ltd, Croydon, Surrey

The paper used in this book is a natural recyclable product made from
wood grown in sustainable forests. The hard coverboard is recycled.

Hodder & Stoughton
A Division of Hodder Headline Ltd
338 Euston Road
London NW1 3BH
www.madaboutbooks.com

Introduction

Cats and dogs are not *supposed* to get on
with each other, let alone live on the same premises in
harmony – but they do. This was agreed upon just after
their equivalent of the Hundred Years' War (known as
'The Great Feline Ferocity') nearly wiped out the pet
population of Europe. A truce was signed which is
adhered to (shakily) in order that both parties can get
the maximum benefit out of doting pet owners.

Tooth-to-claw fighting on the best Axminster
is bound to end in exile for cat or dog or both. So they
have to make the best of it, although this often rankles.
This book illustrates some of the strategies that make it
easier to bear the suppressed wrath that
comes of living with the enemy.

Some dogs don't know what cats are for.

It is difficult for a very small dog to have a *balanced*
friendship with a cat.

Even friendship needs a little spice.

A cat can be a poor audience for a dog's best tricks.

Dogs can sometimes fail to see cat humour.

Well-meaning dogs can be a bit rough…

...something even a friend is unlikely to forget.

There can be mutual affection…

...but a shift in attitude can occur suddenly.

Shared warmth is nice.

On a really cold evening a cat can get quite friendly.

There is often fierce competition for top position.

Jealousy is a terrible thing.

There are no squatters' rights…

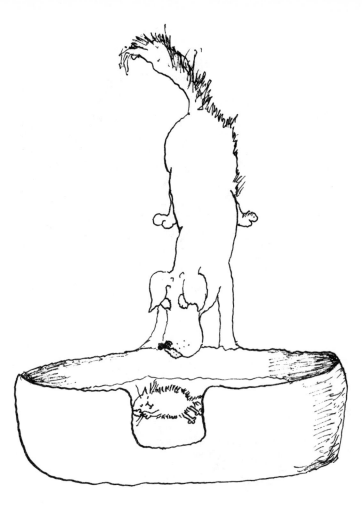

...for anyone.

Dogs like to be playful.

Cats like to be playful.

There's verbal warfare…

...and there's real warfare.

Hostilities can last into the night.

Some cats feel that a day without danger is a day wasted.

An accomplice is a useful distraction.

Dogs do not understand the appeal of fish.

Cats should not underestimate the tenacity
of a small dog.

A cat can be neat, distilled essence of annoyance.

Some dogs have no choice.

Even the toughest dog can feel he is losing the battle.

There's joy in others' discomfort…

…and revenge.

It can be worth going to great lengths to
surprise a friend.

With a friend like this, who needs dental floss?

A tall friend is useful on a wet day.

Teamwork can get results…

...in all locations.

Occasionally, an accomplice needs some extra coaching.

A doggy friend can be handy at times.

Co-operative grooming can go to great lengths.

A friend can comb those hard-to-reach areas.

Dogs can be persuaded to baby-sit.

Cats can make excellent nannies.

A dog's floppy bits can hide something
a cat might be chasing.

Dogs fail to see the point of catching anything
as small as a spider…

...while cats are baffled by dogs taking on things
as big as cars.

Dogs cannot understand why cats hunt such
tiny snacks…

…or try to bite off more than they can chew.

Some dogs find an easier way.

Cats do not get the swimming thing.

To a cat, a tail can look like a twitching mouse.

Best friends often mouse in pairs.

A housemate expects certain standards.

Cats do not usually accompany their friends on walks.

Long grass can be tiring for cats.

Cats like to amuse their friends.

Training is *not* for cats.

Cats pride themselves
on being low-maintenance.

One can roll in a puddle ...

... and then roll on a friend.

A lightweight cat should avoid a heavyweight sneeze.

Where's that cute kitty got to?

Much sport is to be had with professional dog-walkers.

The best hiding place may be close to the enemy...

...but sleeping next to a bulky dog has its dangers.

Some friends tell tales.

Other friends are downright hypocritical.

A cat's best asset is agility.

Small cats can take cover in small places.

If danger looms…

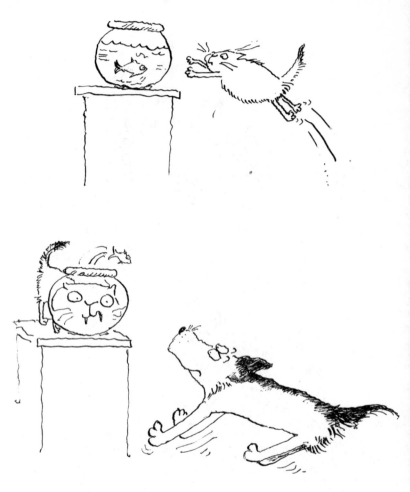

...help can be close by.

On a farm, mercenaries can be hired.

Some dogs may imagine that a tiny cat is
some sort of *hors d'oeuvre*.

Sometimes one's friends let the side down.

Cats have superior claws for going up…

...whereas dogs' claws are better for descending.

It's wise to leave the scene of a crime.

The most visible culprit gets the blame.

Upstaging at the right moment is a fine art.

Cats do not believe in overexertion.

They will always delegate.

Doggy habits can be distasteful.

Dog baiting can be fun and rewarding.

Cats can be surprised by fashion slaves.

Long-haired dogs need extra grooming.

Some dogs will turn drug detective.

A cat is an effective burglar alarm.

Cats are more languid than dogs.

Cats and dogs have a totally different outlook
on car journeys.

An ugly friend is an asset.

Cats may like their housemates but not other dogs.

There is only one cushion.

There are duvet wars...

...and there is only one loser.

Tickle-able tummy competitions are difficult to judge.